BEBOP LICKS
for Piano

BY LES WISE

CONTENTS

T0078936

INTRODUCTION

This book is written for the musician who is interested in acquiring a firm foundation for playing jazz. The ideas presented are from the great musicians who have shaped various facets of the jazz idiom. The developing musician should not merely "memorize licks" but learn to embellish these ideas with his own, forming concepts that ultimately mold an individual style. By building up a vocabulary of these melodic ideas, we can begin connecting them together in endless possibilities to form larger phrases and complete solos.

PLAYBACK+
Speed • Pitch • Balance • Loop

To access audio visit:
www.halleonard.com/mylibrary

2560-2334-5924-6219

ISBN 978-1-4234-6994-0

Copyright © 1982, 2002, 2009 by HAL LEONARD CORPORATION
International Copyright Secured   All Rights Reserved

Visit Hal Leonard Online at
www.halleonard.com

Contact us:
Hal Leonard
7777 West Bluemound Road
Milwaukee, WI 53213
Email: info@halleonard.com

In Europe, contact:
Hal Leonard Europe Limited
42 Wigmore Street
Marylebone, London, W1U 2RN
Email: info@halleonardeurope.com

In Australia, contact:
Hal Leonard Australia Pty. Ltd.
4 Lentara Court
Cheltenham, Victoria, 3192 Australia
Email: info@halleonard.com.au

THE LANGUAGE OF IMPROVISATION

Musical improvisation. Let's define what it is not. It is not the God-given ability to invent melodies from out of the sky. It does not come from a bolt of lightning, enabling one to be a monster soloist. It is not a divine gift which only a few of us have because we are special. What, then, is improvisation? It is **spontaneous reorganization.** Think for a moment of what those two words mean—"the rearrangement of something that already exists." It is learned in much the same way that a language is because musical improvisation is a language. We all have the ability to learn the language of improvisation; it's simply a matter of proper direction.

Let's examine what a language is. When we speak, we do not instantly invent the words which flow from our mouth. They already exist. Likewise, when we solo we use patterns and ideas which already exist in the language of music.

The average high school graduate is said to know about 15,000 words. Yet two individuals may express completely separate ideas, thought, and opinions while using the same set of words. How is this so? Simply by arranging these words in different orders. If we're all operating within the same basic structural vocabulary, then it's the order in which we reorganize the words that give our personality a uniqueness which we call our own.

When we speak, we generally do so intuitively, and it seems to be an automatic process. Yet if we think back and analyze the development of our vocabulary, we see that it really was not. The process of learning to solo is much the same way. Let me point out some of the similarities.

Speech development, up until we entered school, was by imitation. Our parents spoke a word or a phrase, and we simply repeated it. In the same manner, before we ever had a music teacher or knew a thing about music, we simply imitated sounds. We may have heard a melody from a television or radio commercial and attempted to imitate that melody on our instrument.

In the first grade we learned a word. We not only learned how to pronounce the word but how the individual letters symbolize the sounds that form the word. We learned how to spell it and how to write it on the blackboard. To further complicate matters, we had to learn the meaning of the word and how to use it in a sentence. The parallel drawn to our instrument is fairly obvious. In our music lessons we began to learn about some chords, scales, and arpeggios. We learned what notes they consist of, what they sound like, and where they are used. Our test as musicians was to play before an audience—our parents or friends. Our test from our school teacher was to read our story containing our newly learned words to the rest of the class.

With the onset of junior High School, further additions increased our understanding of the English language. I'm sure we all must remember sentence diagramming—now wasn't that just loads of fun? All kinds of lines and arrows were pointing in all directions at words and under words and over words. In complete confusion we thought to ourselves, "So this represents the intuitive speech of one human being communicating to another? How can something so contrived and formulated by any part of just plain everyday communication?" Yet as we learned about our language, the formula became more and more clear, and during the educational process we picked up word after word. One at a time they were added—some from English, some from math, some from history, and some from science. Our vocabulary grew tremendously and usually with much effort.

Now imagine the horror if on your first day of school, the teacher began by handing out enormous books and saying, "Here is a book containing the 15,000 words that you must know by the time you leave the twelfth grade." You would have wanted to go home right then and there. Yet fortunately it didn't happen that way, and instead we learned our language one day at a time. Our verbal communication was a natural, growing, intuitive process.

As word after word was added, the process became so subtle that we now can hardly even remember when and where we learned specific words. Take the word "aluminum" for example. When did you learn it? Was it third grade? fifth grade? eighth grade? Chances are you can't remember. As you went through life acquiring new words, you didn't worry about them, grasp onto them, or hang them around your neck and build your entire life around them. They subtly crept into your vocabulary, and you began to use them intuitively and automatically.

Let's imagine a not so automatic use of communication. Suppose you went to Russia and were suddenly approached by a Russian on the street. The five Russian words you had memorized on the flight over would have to suffice in order to communicate at all. Now don't you think that your speech would sound a bit contrived and mechanical? Would it be at all expressive, intuitive, or automatic? Those five Russian word would be overused, abused, misused, and completely exhausted within one minute. Not to mention the great effort you would employ in an attempt to speak these words in some coherent order. Yet, if you knew 15,000 Russian words, you would simply relax and communicate. The process of how to arrange these words would no longer feel contrived, but completely automatic, or—improvised.

We build our vocabulary on our instruments much as we built our English vocabulary. We slowly and gradually add new licks. Some we may read, some we learn from records, some we copy from a friend. We use what already exists—we copy and imitate. You may ask, "But how can I be original and have my own distinct style if I imitate others?" Well, let me ask you, "Did you reject your first words from your mother and father because you invented your own language?" Of course not. You didn't argue the fact that the object which lifts food into your mouth is called a spoon. Our distinct personality is expressed by the order in which we arrange the words which are common to us all. In music, we may play something that seems completely new and unique. But in reality it's a combination of ideas we already know. It may be four consecutive notes we learned three years ago, combined with part of a lick we took from a record last week. We play this idea and believe that we've stumbled upon something totally new, and in a sense we have. It's a reorganization of that which already existed.

Let's look at another way in which vocabulary is expanded. Have you ever been sitting with a group of friends when somebody used a word that caught your attention? You didn't know the exact meaning of the word, but you knew you had heard it somewhere before, and now by the nature of the sentence your friend used, you understand instantly what the word means. Within this same instant you may have realized you liked the word, made a mental note, of it, then put it completely out of your mind. The next day you were talking to a friend, and "zap"—the same word came out. Once you are proficient at the language of musical improvisation, the same process will happen. You'll step on the bandstand, now knowing what you will play, and the ideas will flow out. You'll remember a lick you heard from a piano player last week and you'll find yourself playing it. You will have learned enough patterns and shapes and combinations of ideas to play this same lick which had been residing in your subconscious mind. Or you may take a few notes of the same lick and combine it with another which you copied from a saxophone player five years earlier. The musical ideas are already in existence, but the way in which you rearrange these ideas will express your own style and personality— just as when you speak. Your unique personality is the order in which you string all the ideas together.

Musical improvisation is a language, just as English, French, Spanish, and German are languages. It has to be learned. Sure it can and will eventually feel natural and "improvised," but it first must be learned in the same contrived manner that we learned our own language or in the same contrived way that we would learn any new language—one word at a time. It sounds free and easy, but is acquired over a lifetime. One new lick or idea at a time—what it is made of, where to use it and what it communicates or expresses. To increase our ability to communicate on our instrument, we increase our musical vocabulary. To increase our musical vocabulary we learn new licks. We play them over and over until they are habits—until our fingers play them independently of our conscious mind—until we can play them in our sleep, with or without our instruments. Repetition. Where do we get them from? Copy records, copy friends, copy friends' records. From transcriptions, from other instruments—one new word or phrase at a time. Then another and another. This is the process by which we learn and expand the language of improvisation.

HOW TO USE THIS BOOK

This book will solve two of the most common problems among musicians. 1)The lack of a strong musical vocabulary (licks, patterns, etc.) and 2)How to connect the ideas into smooth solos once they have been memorized.

You will notice that the book not only contains melodic ideas to be played over individual chord (major, minor, and dominant) but also a great number of larger musical sentences for chord progressions (i.e., IIm7–V7–Imaj7 and turnarounds, i.e., Imaj7–VI7–IIm7–V7).

All the ideas are categorized into sections for easy reference and also the starting note (in interval notation) for every idea is given (root, 3rd, 5th, 7th, etc.). This will enable you to use the ideas more quickly in your playing.

One way to give our solos continuity is to memorize musical sentences. The next step is to connect these sentences into paragraphs. Here's how we do it. In the IIm7–V7–Imaj7 section of the book the melodic ideas are grouped according to the starting note of the IIm7 chord (the root of a Dm7 chord is D, the ♭3rd is F, the 5th is A, etc.) Also notice that the note the IIm7–V7 (Dm7–G7) resolves to when it reaches the Imaj7 (Cmaj7) chord is indicated in interval notation. This is shown because if we wanted to connect the IIm7–V7 line to another progression or add another idea, it's important to know the starting note (interval) of the next idea for it to connect smoothly.

EDITOR'S NOTE: Audio ends at track 82.

MUSICAL EXAMPLES

WORD   SENTENCE

PARAGRAPH

The lines in *Bebop Licks* are written as straight eighth notes for easy reading, but to play the ideas in a "bop" swing fashion the eighth notes should be phrased like this:

Here are some tips for you to think about as you go through the book.

1. Learn small sections at a time, maybe four or eight notes.
2. Play slowly to ensure correct programming of motor skills.
3. Transpose the ideas to all keys.
4. Learn the ideas in different octaves.
5. Practice singing the lines away from your instrument.
6. Record the chord changes and play the ideas against them.
7. Experiment with breaking up the lines rhythmically.
8. Incorporate the ideas into your playing immediately.

MAJOR IDEAS
Starting on the Root

Major Ideas Starting on the Root

MAJOR IDEAS
Starting on the 4th or 11th

MAJOR IDEAS
Starting on the 5th

Major Ideas Starting on the 5th

MAJOR IDEAS
Starting on the 6th or 13th

MAJOR IDEAS
Starting on the 7th

MAJOR IDEAS
Starting on the 2nd or 9th

11

MINOR IDEAS
Starting on the Root

12

Minor Ideas Starting on the Root

MINOR IDEAS
Starting on the ♭3rd

Minor Ideas Starting on the ♭3rd

MINOR IDEAS
Starting on the 4th or 11th

MINOR IDEAS
Starting on the 5th

MINOR IDEAS
Starting on the 6th or 13th

MINOR IDEAS
Starting on the ♭7th

MINOR IDEAS
Starting on the 2nd or 9th

DOMINANT 7TH IDEAS
Starting on the Root

DOMINANT 7TH IDEAS
Starting on the 3rd

Dominant 7th Ideas Starting on the 3rd

DOMINANT 7TH IDEAS
Starting on the 5th

Dominant 7th Ideas Starting on the 5th

DOMINANT 7TH IDEAS
Starting on the ♭7th

Dominant 7th Ideas Starting on the ♭7th

DOMINANT 7TH IDEAS
Starting on the 6th or 13th

27

DOMINANT 7TH IDEAS
Starting on the 2nd or 9th

28

DOMINANT 7TH IDEAS
Starting on the ♭5th

DOMINANT 7TH IDEAS
Starting on the ♯5th

DOMINANT 7TH IDEAS
Starting on the ♭9th

IIm7 V7 Imaj7 IDEAS
Starting on the Root of the IIm7 Chord

IIm7 V7 Imaj7 Starting on the Root of the IIm7 Chord

IIm7 V7 Imaj7 Starting on the Root of the IIm7 Chord

IIm7 V7 Imaj7 Starting on the Root of the IIm7 Chord

IIm7 V7 Imaj7 Starting on the Root of the IIm7 Chord

IIm7 V7 Imaj7 Starting on the Root of the IIm7 Chord

IIm7 V7 Imaj7 Starting on the Root of the IIm7 Chord

IIm7 V7 Imaj7 Starting on the Root of the IIm7 Chord

IIm7 V7 Imaj7 Starting on the Root of the IIm7 Chord

IIm7 V7 Imaj7 Starting on the Root of the IIm7 Chord

IIm7 V7 Imaj7 IDEAS
Starting on the ♭3rd of the IIm7 Chord

IIm7 V7 Imaj7 Starting on the ♭3rd of the IIm7 Chord

IIm7 V7 Imaj7 Starting on the ♭3rd of the IIm7 Chord

IIm7 V7 Imaj7 Starting on the ♭3rd of the IIm7 Chord

IIm7 V7 Imaj7 Starting on the ♭3rd of the IIm7 Chord

IIm7 V7 Imaj7 Starting on the ♭3rd of the IIm7 Chord

IIm7 V7 Imaj7 Starting on the ♭3rd of the IIm7 Chord

IIm7 V7 Imaj7 Starting on the ♭3rd of the IIm7 Chord

IIm7 V7 Imaj7 Starting on the ♭3rd of the IIm7 Chord

IIm7 V7 Imaj7 Starting on the ♭3rd of the IIm7 Chord

IIm7 V7 Imaj7 Starting on the ♭3rd of the IIm7 Chord

IIm7 V7 Imaj7 IDEAS
Starting on the 4th or 11th of the IIm7 Chord

IIm7 V7 Imaj7 Starting on the 4th or 11th of the IIm7 Chord

IIm7 V7 Imaj7 Starting on the 4th or 11th of the IIm7 Chord

IIm7 V7 Imaj7 Starting on the 4th or 11th of the IIm7 Chord

IIm7 V7 Imaj7 IDEAS
Starting on the 5th of the IIm7 Chord

IIm7 V7 Imaj7 Starting on the 5th of the IIm7 Chord

IIm7 V7 Imaj7 Starting on the 5th of the IIm7 Chord

IIm7 V7 Imaj7 Starting on the 5th of the IIm7 Chord

IIm7 V7 Imaj7 Starting on the 5th of the IIm7 Chord

IIm7 V7 Imaj7 IDEAS
Starting on the 6th or 13th of the IIm7 Chord

IIm7 V7 Imaj7 Starting on the 6th or 13th of the IIm7 Chord

IIm7 V7 Imaj7 IDEAS
Starting on the ♭7th of the IIm7 Chord

IIm7 V7 Imaj7 IDEAS
Starting on the 2nd or 9th of the IIm7 Chord

IIm7 V7 Imaj7 Starting on the 2nd or 9th of the IIm7 Chord

IIm7 V7 Imaj7 Starting on the 2nd or 9th of the IIm7 Chord

IIm7 V7 Imaj7 Starting on the 2nd or 9th of the IIm7 Chord

IIm7 V7 Imaj7 Starting on the 2nd or 9th of the IIm7 Chord

IIm7 V7 Imaj7 Starting on the 2nd or 9th of the IIm7 Chord

IIm7 V7 IDEAS
Starting on the Root of the IIm7 Chord

IIm7 V7 Starting on the Root of the IIm7 Chord

IIm7 V7 IDEAS
Starting on the ♭3rd of the IIm7 Chord

IIm7 V7 IDEAS
Starting on the 4th or 11th of the IIm7 Chord

IIm7 V7 IDEAS
Starting on the 5th of the IIm7 Chord

IIm7 V7 IDEAS
Starting on the 6th or 13th of the IIm7 Chord

IIm7 V7 IDEAS
Starting on the ♭7th of the IIm7 Chord

IIm7 V7 IDEAS
Starting on the 2nd or 9th of the IIm7 Chord

TURNAROUNDS
Starting on the Root of the Imaj7 Chord

TURNAROUNDS
Starting on the 3rd of the Imaj7 Chord

TURNAROUNDS
Starting on the 5th of the Imaj7 Chord

Turnarounds Starting on the 5th of the Imaj7 Chord

IDEA SUBSTITUTION CHART

PLAY ANY

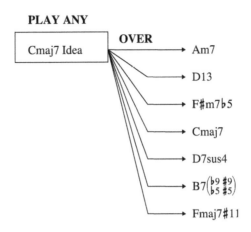

Cmaj7 Idea **OVER**
→ Am7
→ D13
→ F#m7♭5
→ Cmaj7
→ D7sus4
→ B7$\left(\begin{smallmatrix}♭9 & \#9\\♭5 & \#5\end{smallmatrix}\right)$
→ Fmaj7#11

PLAY ANY

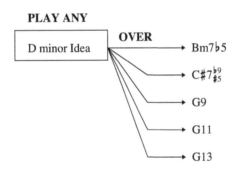

D minor Idea **OVER**
→ Bm7♭5
→ C#7$^{♭9}_{\#5}$
→ G9
→ G11
→ G13

PLAY ANY

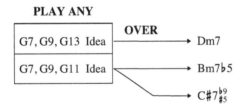

G7, G9, G13 Idea **OVER**
→ Dm7

G7, G9, G11 Idea
→ Bm7♭5
→ C#7$^{♭9}_{\#5}$

ABOUT THE AUTHOR

For decades, Les Wise has been gaining recognition as one of the nation's outstanding guitarists...and that recognition is well deserved.

Les was born in the Spring of 1948 in New Orleans, Louisiana. His musical training began twelve years later when he picked up the guitar. During his early years, Les studied with Joe Pass, John Gray, and Roger Filiberto, so by th time he entered the Naval School of Music in 1965, he was well prepared.

After spending most of his four years in the Navy as a member of the Naval Band, Les received an Honorable Discharge and settled in Chicago. It was here that some big name band leaders began to notice this talented, young musician. In only two years in Chicago, Les performed in the bands of Les Brown, David Rose, Woody Herman (behind singer Jack Jones), and Harry James.

Toward the end of 1970, Les was wooed away from the Chicago jazz scene to go on the road as Musical Director for variety performer John Bach. After two years of touring, Les returned to his hometown of New Orleans. It wasn't long before word of the now experienced Wise was all over town. In no time at all, Les Wise was recognized as one of the top musicians in the "birthplace of jazz." When a guitarist was needed anywhere in town, it was a pretty sure bet that the phone at the Wise household would be ringing.

This notoriety gave Les an opportunity to branch out into many new areas. Local producers began to use him on many recording sessions, including commercial jingle dates for Ford Motor Company, American Motors, Gulf-Western, Lever Brothers, Alka-Seltzer, The National Football League, Sunkist, E.F. Hutton, IBM, Bell Telephone, Exxon, and Standard oil. Local educators also realized that Les' experience could be useful in the classroom. As it turned out, Les proved to be particularly skillful at conveying his experience to younger players, and he was hired as a resident instructor at Loyola University in New Orleans.

Having conquered all of the musical plateaus of New Orleans, Les decided in 1977 to take his family to the West Coast. Not surprisingly, his talents were again immediately noticed. In Los Angeles, he began playing with many jazz greats, including Leroy Vinnegar, Sherman Ferguson, Joe Diorio, Eugene Wright, Jack McDuff, Ernie Watts, Jimmy Smith, Max Roach, Willie Bobo, Ronnie Foster, Harold Land, Dwight Dickerson, Bob Maze, Joe Sample, Bob Magnusson, Roy McCurdy, Ted Hawk, and Howard Roberts. It was Howard Roberts who also discovered Les' talents as an educator and hired him as a staff instructor at the Guitar Institute of Technology (G.I.T.).

In a town already bursting at the seams with talented guitarists, Les had no trouble breaking into the studios. His guitar work was heard on radio and television for Levi's Jeans, Coca-Cola, 7-Up, Max Factor, Von's Market, Alpha Beta Markets, and Ralph's. The West Coast music community really took notice when Les was named the outstanding act at the 1978 Orange County Jazz Festival.

Les Wise is known and respected across the country as an outstanding musician, educator, and author of *Inner Jazz*, *Bebop Bible*, co-author of *Ten*, and columnist in *International Musician and Recording World*. There really is no way to describe his technical skill and musical sensitivity. To fully appreciate the kind of musician he is, you have to hear him play.